McCavity

Dee Kay

McCavity was banished from Tooth Fairy Town and constantly plots to take back control of it.

Dee Kay, McCavity's son, is quite dull and clumsy, but he wants to be just like his father.

Library of Congress Cataloging-in-Publication Data

Olberg, Henry, 1951-
 The magical tooth fairies : the secret of the magic dust / by Henry Olberg.
       p. cm.
    Audience: K to grade 3.
 Summary: "The tooth fairies Lynn, Leo Lino, Basta, and Professor discover the magic found in baby teeth and demonstrate the importance of keeping teeth clean and healthy"-- Provided by publisher.
    ISBN 978-0-86715-567-9
 1. Teeth--Care and hygiene--Juvenile literature. 2. Deciduous teeth--Juvenile literature. I. Title. II. Title: Secret of the magic RK63.O53 2012
      617.6'01--dc23
                                2012010151

© 2012 Quintessence Publishing Co, Inc

5 4 3 2 1

Quintessence Publishing Co Inc
4350 Chandler Drive
Hanover Park, IL 60133
www.quintpub.com

All rights reserved. This book or any part thereof may not be reproduced, stored in a retrieval system, or transmitted in any form or by any means, electronic, mechanical, photocopying, or otherwise, without prior written permission of the publisher.

Production date: 10-1-2012
Printed by Everbest Printing Company (Guangzhou, China), Co. Ltd
Job Batch #: 110929.1

Editor: Leah Huffman
Production: Angelina Sanchez
Printed in China

Quintessence Publishing Co, Inc

Chicago, Berlin, Tokyo, London, Paris, Milan, Barcelona, Beijing, Istanbul, Moscow, New Delhi, Prague, São Paulo, Seoul, Singapore, and Warsaw

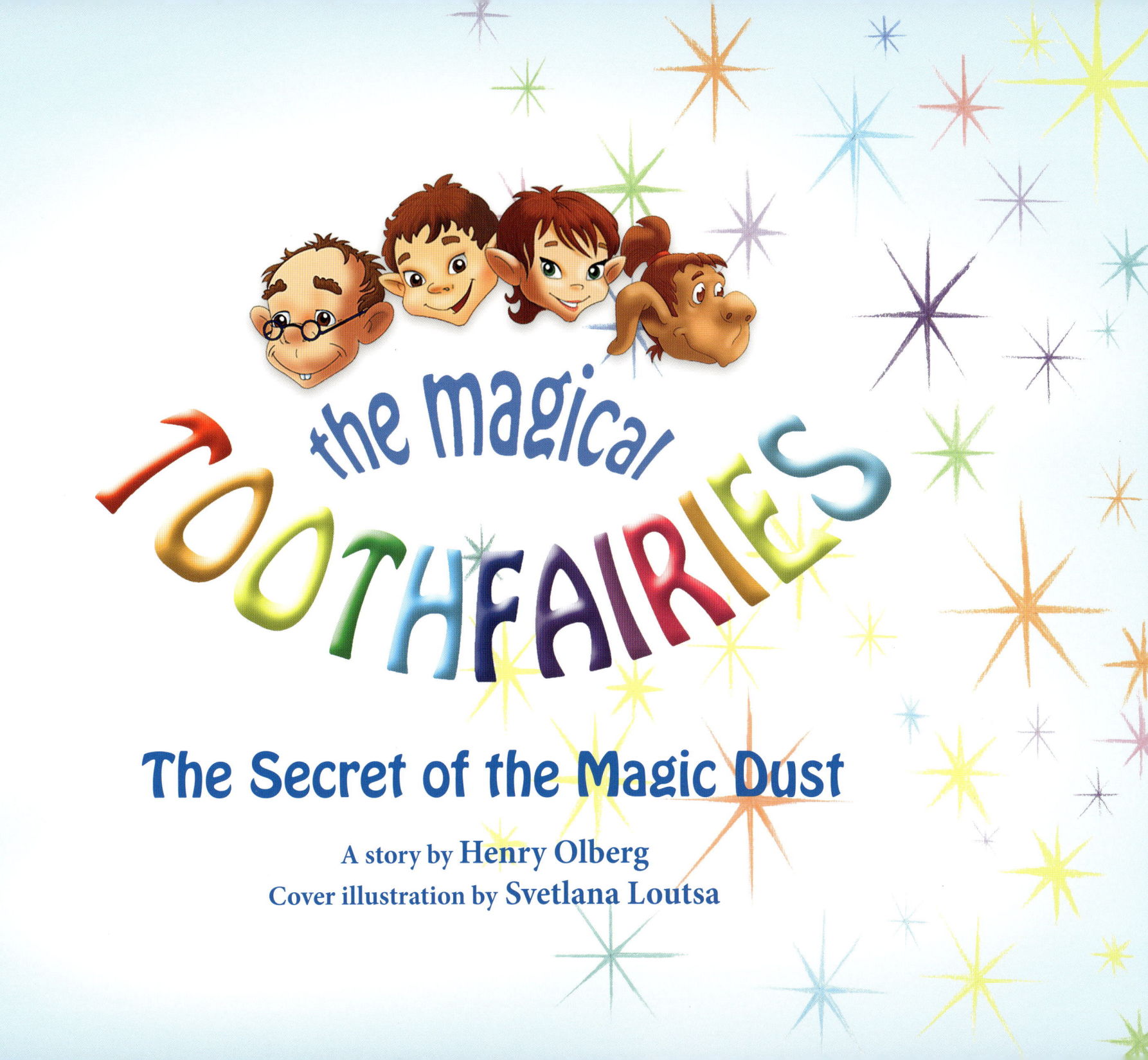

the magical TOOTHFAIRIES

The Secret of the Magic Dust

A story by **Henry Olberg**

Cover illustration by **Svetlana Loutsa**

High above the clouds—much higher still than that—the home of the tooth fairies lies nestled near the stars. And if you have never heard of Tooth Fairy Town, perhaps you have at least imagined it or even caught a glimpse of its colors and shine.

Look closely now. Can you see the fairies? Hidden right here?

How long have they been there, you ask? Only always. That is, as long as there have been children to attend to and important work to do:

Whenever a child loses her first baby tooth, the tooth fairies secretly and quietly come to her bed. They collect that beautiful white jewel and carry it to their mystical city. In exchange for a clean-scrubbed baby tooth, the fairies leave a present—a coin—under her pillow. One day, the tooth fairies will visit you, too. And if you rub this coin at night before you go to bed, a shooting star will fall from the sky. Right at that moment, you can make a wish.

You must remember one very important thing, though. Tooth fairies will only collect teeth that children have taken good care of. If they find a dirty tooth or one with a hole in it, they leave a toothbrush and toothpaste instead of a coin to remind you to always brush your teeth nice and clean.

Now you might ask why the fairies collect children's baby teeth at all.

The answer is quite simple: The teeth contain the children's dreams, hopes, and desires. And when the tooth mills of Tooth Fairy Town grind them to dust, this dust has magical powers. If it is strewn over the tooth fairies, the magical powers get passed on to them.

The tooth fairies also pour the magic dust into their drinking water system, which is why they never get sick. In fact, they live forever.

So you can understand now why your carefully cleaned baby teeth are so important to the tooth fairies: Dirty teeth hold no powers and are of no value.

However, Tooth Fairy Town has not always been as beautiful as it is today, and the fairies have not always been so cheerful and healthy. There once was a time long, long ago when tooth fairies lacked the magic of the mill dust. They had to work hard, climbing down the sky ladder to collect the children's teeth and then climbing up again, their backpacks full and heavy with their night's labor.

McCavity, the mayor during these troubling years, found joy in the fairies' misery and delighted in the city's destruction. He knew the danger of sugary sweets and did his evil best to poison the fairies. And the candy wrappers that lay scattered about the streets, making an otherwise beautiful city ugly and dirty, were only part of the proof that the mayor's plan was succeeding.

Life in Tooth Fairy Town was difficult, and the fairies barely managed to retrieve the children's teeth, let alone fulfill their wishes. Such failure made the fairies very sad. They knew something had to happen—something had to change—if they were to save their city and themselves. And since they were fairies first and foremost, they made sure something did happen. It all began like this....

One day, Lynn headed out for a walk to look for her friends Leo Lino, Basta, and Professor. She found them sitting on a narrow bridge, their legs dangling over the side and their shoulders hunched as they stared into the slow-flowing gray-green water beneath them.

"You look as if you couldn't lift a finger!" Lynn said.

Professor glanced up and sighed, dark circles under his tired eyes. "That's the way it is. Look around us, Lynn! It's this candy McCavity has strewn everywhere. It may as well be poison for what it does to us."

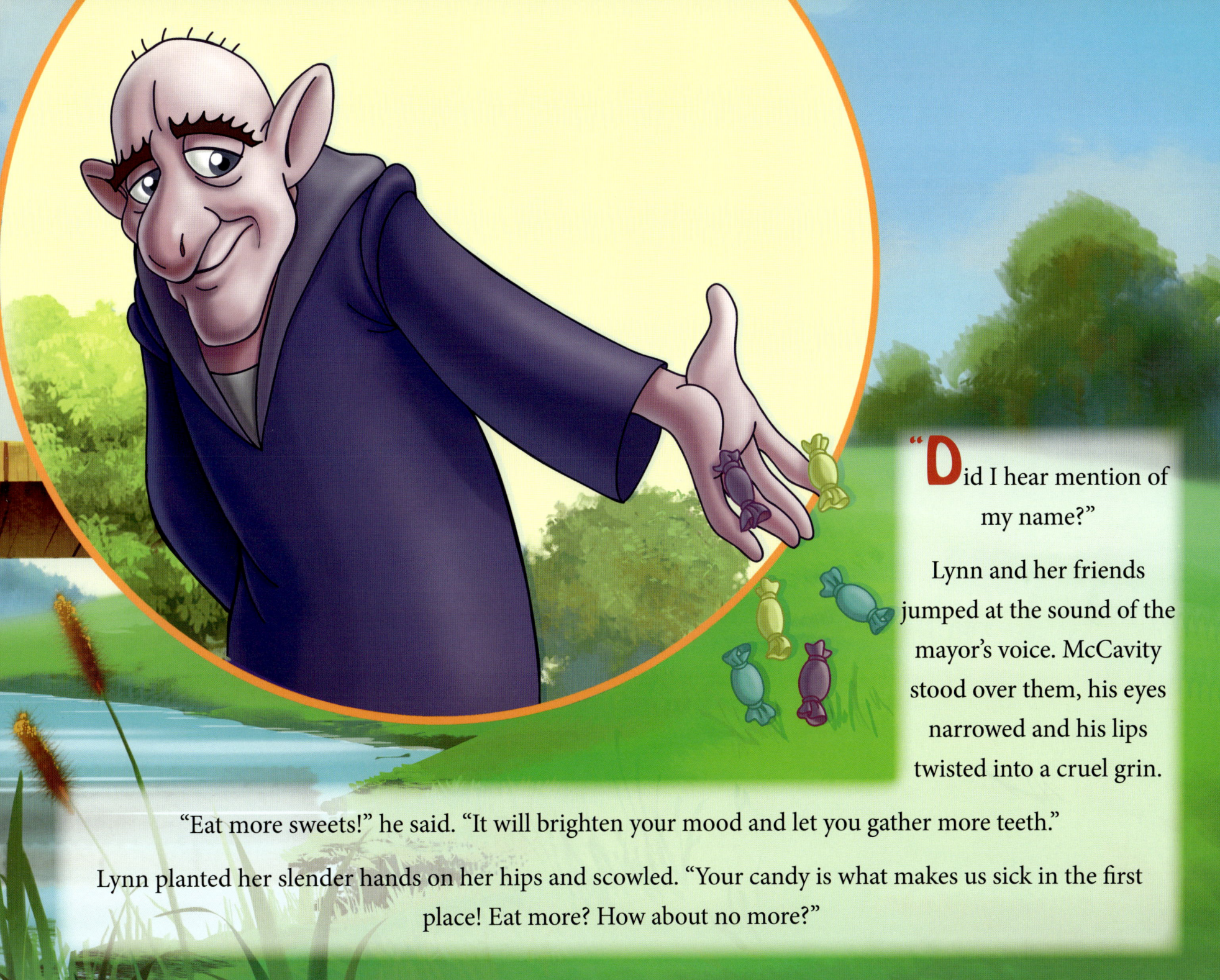

"Did I hear mention of my name?"

Lynn and her friends jumped at the sound of the mayor's voice. McCavity stood over them, his eyes narrowed and his lips twisted into a cruel grin.

"Eat more sweets!" he said. "It will brighten your mood and let you gather more teeth."

Lynn planted her slender hands on her hips and scowled. "Your candy is what makes us sick in the first place! Eat more? How about no more?"

McCavity chuckled as he rummaged underneath his wide cape and then tossed a handful of sweets toward the fairies. Basta immediately snatched at them, but Professor managed to take the candy away just in time.

McCavity smiled triumphantly.

"Rubbish!" he said. "Just look how good it tastes! Even Basta grabs what he can get his hands on." He turned around and shuffled away, his cackling laughter echoing behind him.

Lynn glared at Basta. "If you suck on one more candy, you are no longer my friend. We have to stop eating the mayor's awful candy. All of us have to stop!"

Basta's eyes widened, and then he hung his head in shame.

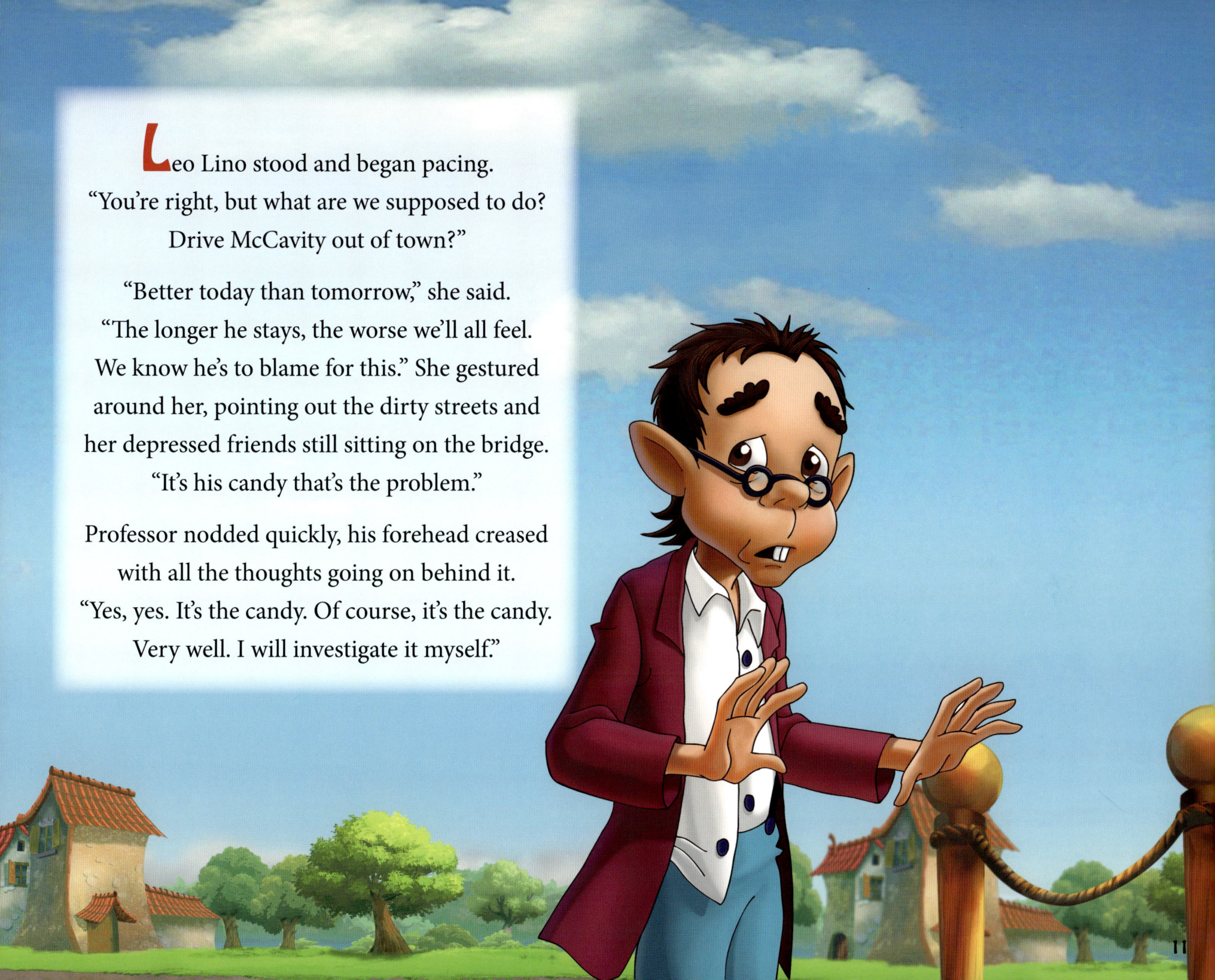

Leo Lino stood and began pacing. "You're right, but what are we supposed to do? Drive McCavity out of town?"

"Better today than tomorrow," she said. "The longer he stays, the worse we'll all feel. We know he's to blame for this." She gestured around her, pointing out the dirty streets and her depressed friends still sitting on the bridge. "It's his candy that's the problem."

Professor nodded quickly, his forehead creased with all the thoughts going on behind it. "Yes, yes. It's the candy. Of course, it's the candy. Very well. I will investigate it myself."

Back in his laboratory, Professor rushed around in a frenzy of beakers and test tubes. He boiled the candies, weighed them, measured them, shook and sniffed them. The liquids hissed and shot off plumes of colorful smoke so foul smelling that his friends sneezed and coughed as they rubbed their eyes and held their noses.

"Astounding!" Professor finally shouted. "Truly astounding!"

"What is it?" Lynn asked, her voice full of eagerness.

"The blue sweets...." He held one up—and well out of reach of poor Basta, who looked as if he could hardly keep himself from grabbing for it. "They make you feel faint and sleepy. The green ones," he added, "destroy your teeth and bones." Then he picked up a red one, holding it carefully as if it might bite him.

"But these are the most dangerous of all because they make you lose your temper for no reason at all— even with your friends. Worse yet, if you combine the three candies, eating them one after the other, you'll only want to eat more and more." He paused as he shook his head. "It becomes impossible to stop eating them."

Lynn gasped. "Impossible to stop?" The friends looked at each other, fear in their eyes. "If that's the case, we may as well admit we can't think for ourselves. And then what are we to do? Tooth fairies who can't think for themselves? It's unheard of!"

But Professor wouldn't have been Professor if he hadn't already started searching for a cure. "I've had a wonderful idea," he said. His eyes shone as he held out some candies his friends had never seen before. "New sweets made of our wholesome Zedion fruit. They taste much better and they're healthy. Instead of stealing your strength and energy, they give you even more. Try some!"

Looking a little unsure but still eager for something sweet, Basta popped one of Professor's Zedion candies into his mouth.

Basta beamed at the other tooth fairies.

"A success!" Professor said with relief.

Lynn and Leo Lino tried the new candy, and their smiles said they were just as delighted with them as Basta was. "Definitely a success," Lynn agreed.

"Come on! We have to tell Mayer!" Lynn called to Basta and Leo Lino as she raced out the door. "Thank you, Professor!"

The trio shouted for their friend Mayer, McCavity's brother. They found him scouring the town, checking whether the evil mayor was still distributing candies. "You must come with us at once, Mayer," Lynn said. "We have to show you something!"

Back at his lab, Professor stood bent over a drawing when his friends burst through the door, Mayer following close behind them.

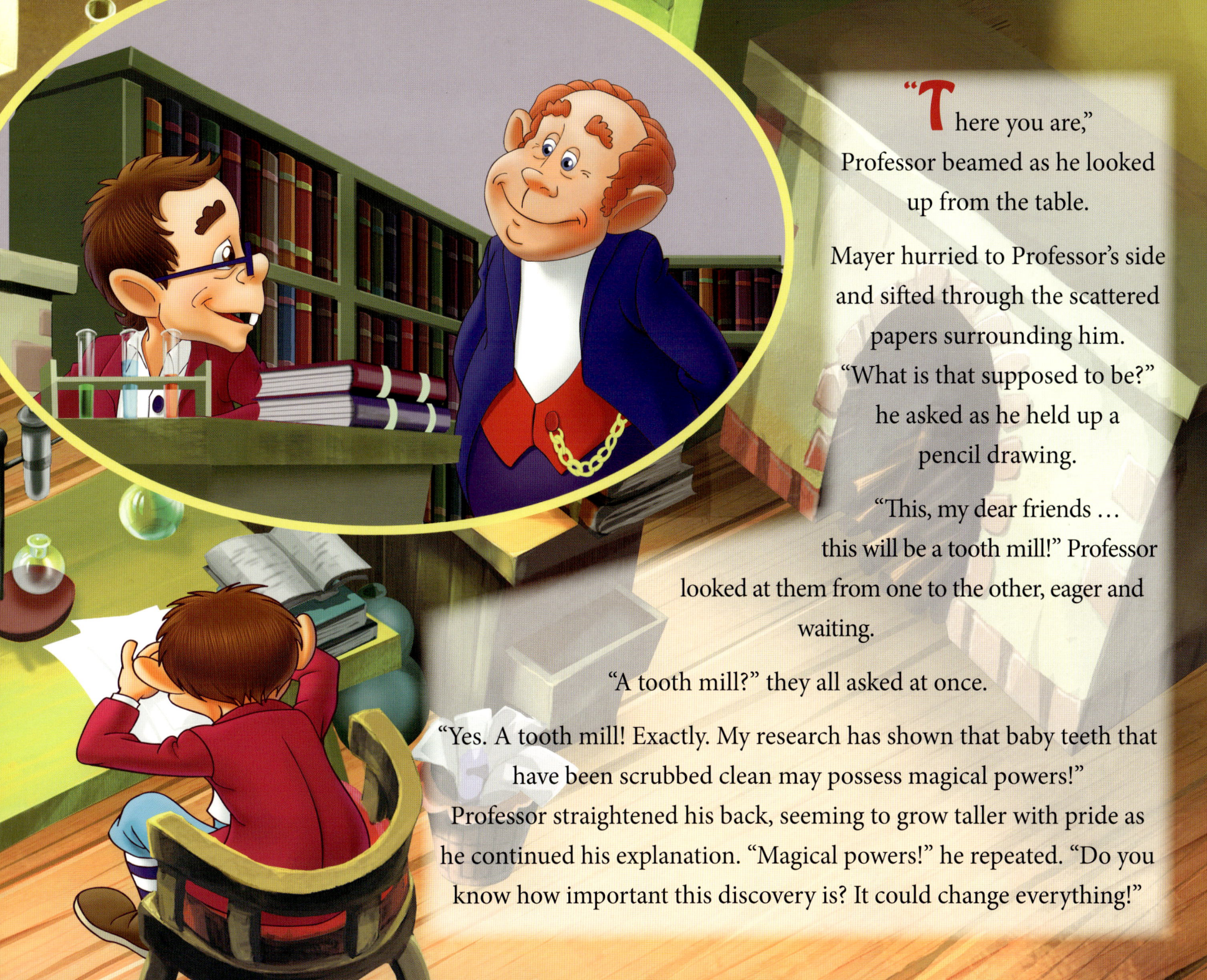

"There you are," Professor beamed as he looked up from the table.

Mayer hurried to Professor's side and sifted through the scattered papers surrounding him. "What is that supposed to be?" he asked as he held up a pencil drawing.

"This, my dear friends … this will be a tooth mill!" Professor looked at them from one to the other, eager and waiting.

"A tooth mill?" they all asked at once.

"Yes. A tooth mill! Exactly. My research has shown that baby teeth that have been scrubbed clean may possess magical powers!" Professor straightened his back, seeming to grow taller with pride as he continued his explanation. "Magical powers!" he repeated. "Do you know how important this discovery is? It could change everything!"

"Wait a minute!" Mayer interrupted. "Magical powers, you say? That's exactly what I saw in my dream last night. This can't be a coincidence!"

Leo Lino raised an eyebrow in suspicion. "What did you dream about?"

"I saw a large mill in Tooth Fairy Town that grinds children's baby teeth to dust." He rubbed his chin in thought. "And, well, the snow-white dust had—believe it or not, it was just as Professor said—powers. The dust worked magic when sprinkled on a fairy's head."

Professor jumped to his feet. "That's it! That's the solution! Sprinkle magic dust on heads. If we stop eating McCavity's candy, we can think for ourselves again. And if we think for ourselves again, we can build this mill, use the fairy dust, and banish the mayor from his office and then from town."

"We'll start building the tooth mill immediately," Leo Lino said as a smile spread wide across his face. "Everything will finally be all right!"

Construction of the tooth mill began right away. All of the tooth fairies stopped eating McCavity's sweets, so they had a lot of energy.

As more and more friends joined in on the construction of the mill, McCavity couldn't help but notice the busy goings-on. The town was swarming with tooth fairies full of energy and hope. "What's the meaning of this?" he demanded. "Why am I, the mayor, not informed? Who has given you permission to build this mill? And…." He took a deep breath as the anger boiled in him. "Why doesn't anybody like my sweets anymore?"

But McCavity wouldn't have been McCavity if he hadn't hatched a plan of sabotage. "We'll regain control of the fairies and the town," he said as he glanced at his son, Dee Kay. "You are going to hide an old rag in the drive shaft of the mill. Then when the fairies try to start the mill, it will break, and they will all see what happens when they sneak around behind the mayor's back."

His father's plan frightened Dee Kay. But he was more afraid to be disobedient, so he did as McCavity ordered.

Finally, the big day of the mill opening arrived.

"Everything will function perfectly," Professor assured his worried friends. "And the magic dust will make us immortal!"

"Immortal," Mayer said with a satisfied smile. "Isn't this all so wonderful?"

"But first," Lynn said with excitement, "we have another surprise. And it's a big one!"

"You will be our new mayor!" Leo Lino jumped in, too eager for patience.

"And McCavity will be sent to Nastian," Lynn continued, "where he can't do any more harm to us."

Mayer shook his head in confusion. "But that's impossible! McCavity is the mayor …and my brother!"

"Yes, it is possible!" Professor handed Mayer a long list of signatures. "The tooth fairies have voted unanimously for you to become their new mayor from today on. You can't refuse."

Still numb with surprise, Mayer looked at the long list of names. "But…."

"No buts!" Basta grinned. "Accept the vote and send McCavity into the forests of Nastian."

Mayer realized his friends were right—no buts and no excuses. Everyone had voted him in as the new mayor. So he set off to meet McCavity.

McCavity and Dee Kay backed away startled as Mayer entered their house. When Mayer began to explain about the signatures and his brother's discharge as mayor, McCavity couldn't contain his anger. "You?" he said with a sneer as he glared at his brother. "The new mayor?"

But Mayer remained calm and continued to read aloud what the town had decided. "You have two hours to leave Tooth Fairy Town. You—meaning the both of you," he said as he glanced from his brother to his nephew, "you can make a new home in Nastian!"

His face red with rage, McCavity threw the mayor's necklace at his brother and stormed out of his house.

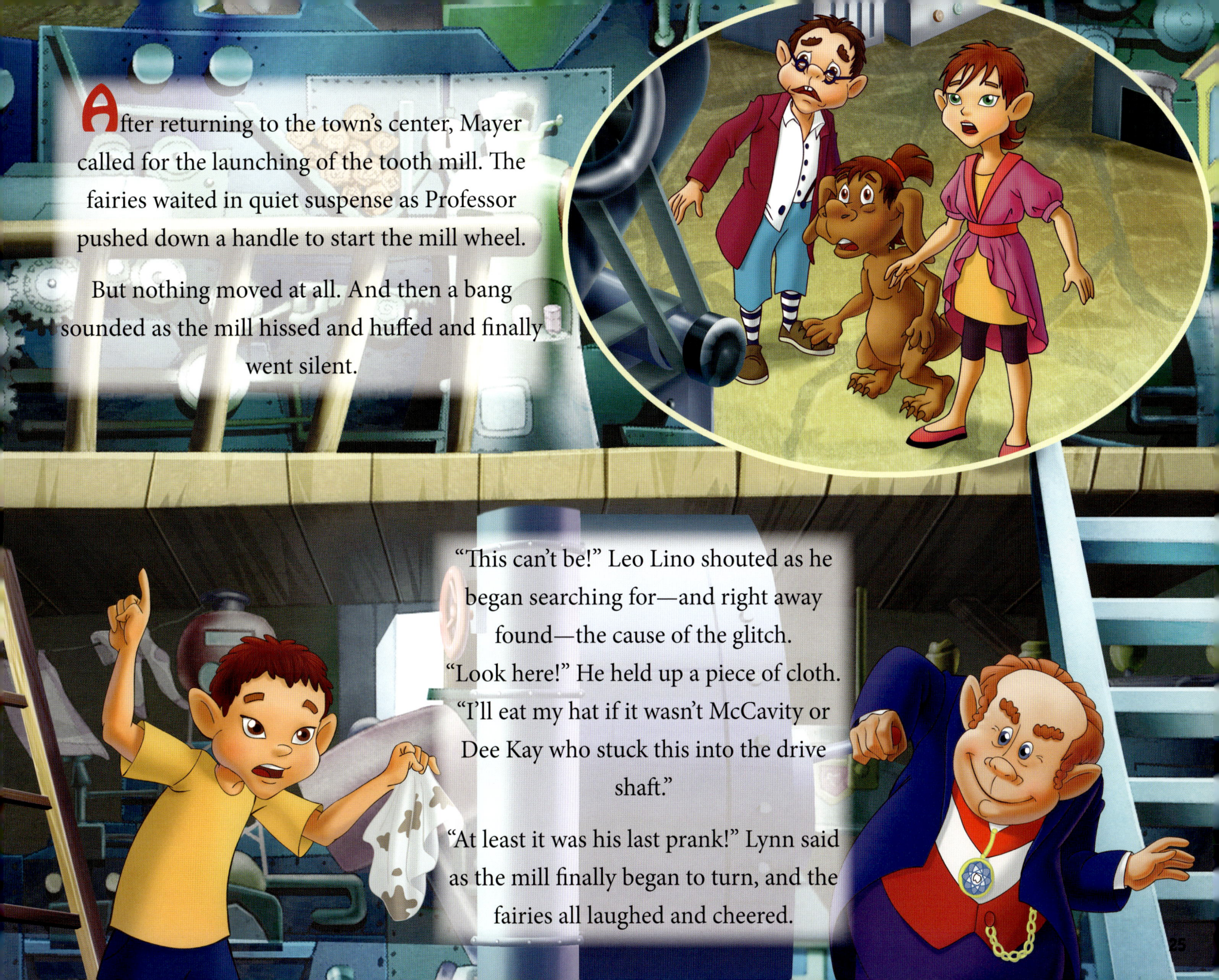

After returning to the town's center, Mayer called for the launching of the tooth mill. The fairies waited in quiet suspense as Professor pushed down a handle to start the mill wheel.

But nothing moved at all. And then a bang sounded as the mill hissed and huffed and finally went silent.

"This can't be!" Leo Lino shouted as he began searching for—and right away found—the cause of the glitch.

"Look here!" He held up a piece of cloth. "I'll eat my hat if it wasn't McCavity or Dee Kay who stuck this into the drive shaft."

"At least it was his last prank!" Lynn said as the mill finally began to turn, and the fairies all laughed and cheered.

As the first pile of white tooth dust began forming in the catch bin, a hush fell over the town. Mayer took up a handful and looked at his four friends who had helped the fairies reach this moment. Pinching a small bit between his fingers, he sprinkled the dust over their heads.

"Ooooooooooh!" the crowd whispered in awe. Thousands of tiny stars glittered over the four friends' heads. Then the impossible happened:

Over Leo Lino's head, the image of an excited little red-haired girl appeared, her face lit up with the excitement of losing her first tooth. "Wow! Did you see that?" Leo Lino exclaimed.

Lynn raised her arms, and Mayer began to float as if lifted by an invisible hand. He paddled the air, frantically trying to regain his balance. As Lynn slowly lowered her arms, Mayer found himself on his own two feet again.

"Isn't that terrific?" Lynn clapped her hands in delight. "I can move anything simply with the force of my mind."

Then, without warning, Professor vanished and reappeared in front of a strange house. As he hovered in the air, he peered through a window and discovered a baby tooth lying next to the pillow of a sleeping child—the same little girl that had appeared in the image over Leo Lino's head. Professor nodded his head once and—bam!—he was next to his friends in Tooth Fairy Town again.

"I can beam myself to any place on earth!" he said, quite full of happy wonder.

As for Basta, green light rays shot out of his eyes. He startled even himself. "Wow! I can see through walls!"

Professor watched all of his friends discovering their new powers. "Isn't this all just so grand," he said with a contented sigh.

The first mission followed immediately. The tooth fairies stood beside the bed of a young boy named Ben. Professor first made sure the child was sleeping, and then Leo Lino took the tooth from under the pillow while Basta laid a coin in its place. As the fairies disappeared, Ben awoke to find his first wishing coin—his reward for brushing his tooth clean. He held the shiny coin tight in his hands and then rubbed it, spraying sparks across his bedroom. At the very same moment, a star shot across the sky and Ben made his wish.

... **A**nd all of this has been happening for years and years—many more than you could ever care to count. And just as children rely on the tooth fairies to make their wishes come true, the fairies rely on the children for the magic that makes it all possible.

For without clean-brushed teeth, there would be no magic dust.

So now you know their story. And now you know your role in their story: Do your very best to take care of your teeth, and the fairies will do their very best to take care of your wishes.

Why are these children smiling?

They belong to the . . .

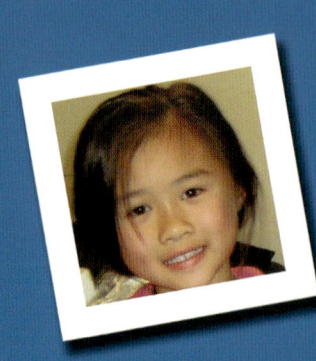

Become a Real ToothFairy
www.AmericasToothFairy.org

America's ToothFairy Kids Club!

Sign up today!

Receive personal letters from the ToothFairy and fun activities for a beautiful smile!

...because every child deserves a healthy smile.®

www.AmericasToothFairyKids.org

In the next book, read as evil McCavity and his son, Dee Kay, plot to once again take control of Tooth Fairy Town.

McCavity hatches a plan to make his own tooth dust with magical powers. But without a proper tooth mill or clean-scrubbed baby teeth, both of which belong only to the tooth fairies, he'll have to collect the rotten, unbrushed teeth and grind them into dust himself.

But will his plan succeed? Well, what do you think?

In the meantime, the tooth fairies are in Mexico to help a little boy trying desperately to catch two parrots that have stolen his first baby tooth.